Bridgestone
B O O K S

World of Reptiles

Bearded Dragons

by Jason Glaser

Consultants:
Staff of the Reptile Gardens
Rapid City, South Dakota

Capstone
press

Mankato, Minnesota

Bearded Dragons

A hungry **dingo** spots a bearded dragon resting in the sun. The dingo tries to grab the dragon and eat it. But the dragon puffs up its beard and opens its mouth wide to look bigger. The dingo is scared away and the dragon is safe.

Although they can look fierce, bearded dragons are usually friendly toward people. These small lizards are popular as reptile pets.

Bearded dragons are related to iguanas and frilled-neck lizards. Like most reptiles, bearded dragons hatch from eggs, are covered with scales, and are **cold-blooded**.

◀ Bearded dragons climb up on sunny rocks to stay warm.

6

What Bearded Dragons Look Like

Bearded dragons are named for their dark throat pouch. When they are scared, the pouch fills with air and puffs out. Small scales on the pouch look like spikes on the skin's surface. The dragons look like they have beards.

Bearded dragons have short, colorful bodies and flat, triangle-shaped heads. Adult dragons are 1 to 2 feet (0.3 to 0.6 meters) long. Their skin is a mix of gray, red, brown, tan, or gold.

◀ Bearded dragons have short, flat bodies, short legs, and a long, thick tail.

Bearded Dragon Range Map

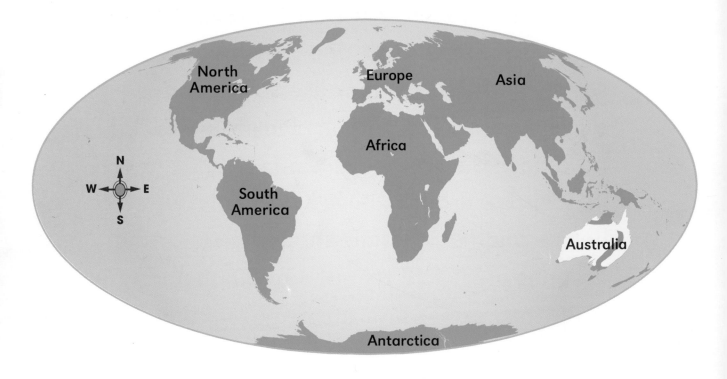

Where Wild Bearded Dragons Live

Bearded Dragons in the World

Wild bearded dragons make their home in Australia. All seven **species** live there. They can be found on most of the continent.

Many bearded dragons live as pets in Europe and North America. These dragons are **descendants** of lizards that were taken illegally from Australia. Thousands of bearded dragons are hatched and sold in pet stores every year.

Bearded Dragon Habitats

Bearded dragons usually live in the **scrublands** and wooded areas of Australia. They like to rest on rocks, tree limbs, or fallen branches. Some bearded dragons live at the edges of Australia's hot deserts.

Bearded dragons dig **burrows** in the ground. They stay underground on hot days. During cool weather, bearded dragons sometimes become **dormant**. They sleep in their burrows for two to three months.

◀ Bearded dragons live where they can stay warm in the sun and cool in the shade.

What Bearded Dragons Eat

Bearded dragons eat anything they can get. Food is hard to find where they live. They munch on insects, leaves, and small plants. Dragons also snack on rodents and tiny lizards.

Bearded dragons are hunters. They snatch up small creatures on the ground or in trees. They gobble up and swallow their **prey** whole.

◀ A grasshopper makes a tasty meal for this bearded dragon.

Dangers to Bearded Dragons

Dingoes, large lizards, and other **predators** eat bearded dragons. When in danger, dragons puff up their beards and open their mouths wide. They look much bigger than they really are. Sometimes predators are scared away.

Pet dragons can face danger too. When their owners don't give them the proper food or heat, the dragons may die.

Even though they are small, bearded dragons are strong lizards. They will continue to live in the wild and as popular reptile pets.

◄ Bearded dragons make themselves appear larger and more fierce to scare away predators.

Index